NICKNAMES PAST AND PRESENT

ABOUT THE AUTHOR

Christine Rose, CG, CGL, FASG, is a Certified Genealogist, a Certified Genealogical Lecturer, and full-time professional genealogist. She was elected Fellow, American Society of Genealogists, an honor bestowed by peers based on quantity and quality of publications, and limited to only fifty at any time. She was the recipient of the prestigious Donald Lines Jacobus award for two genealogy books. Her background as compiler of numerous genealogies and articles; an Associate of the Board for Certification of Genealogists; former Vice President of Association of Professional Genealogists and of the Federation of Genealogical Societies, and longtime columnist for the latter's *Forum* have all contributed to a productive career in the field of genealogy. Christine, well known as a lecturer, has presented at national and regional conferences, at the National Institute of Historical Research in Washington, D.C., and is on the faculty of the Samford University Institute of Genealogy and Historical Research in Birmingham. She is also founder of the Rose Family Association and its editor since its inception. Her articles have appeared in national journals and magazines. As an author, her books include the highly praised *Courthouse Research for Family Historians: Your Guide to Genealogical Treasures; Genealogical Proof Standard: Building a Solid Case; Courthouse Indexes Illustrated; Family Associations, Organization and Management*; and others. She is also co-author of the popular *Complete Idiot's Guide to Genealogy*, now in its second edition.

NICKNAMES

Past and Present

A list of nicknames for given names used in the past and present time

5th Edition Expanded

And including
Appendix A: Dutch and Frisian given names with English equivalents
Appendix B: English given names with Dutch and Frisian equivalents
Appendix C: Truncated/Superscripted Names
Appendix D: Names used by both males and females
Appendix E: A reprint of an article by Donald Lines Jacobus, Ph.D, FASG
and introducing in this edition
Appendix F: Italian given names and their English equivalents, nicknames, and diminutives

Compiled by
Christine Rose, CG, CGL, FASG

SAN JOSE, CALIFORNIA
2007

ISBN 978-0929626185

First edition 1987, 2nd edition 1995,
3rd edition 1998, 4th edition 2002,
5th edition 2007

10 9 8 7 6 5 4 3 2 1

Published by: CR Publications, 1474 Montelegre Dr., San Jose, CA 95120

Printed by Thomson Shore, Inc., Dexter, Michigan
Author's email: Christine4Rose@cs.com
Author's website: www.Christine4Rose.com

Cover design by Ann Silberlicht of Silberlicht Studio

CONTENTS

Other Books by this Author

Courthouse Research for Family Historians
Genealogical Proof Standard
Courthouse Indexes Illustrated
Military Pension Laws 1776-1858
Family Associations: Organization and Management
The Brothers Rev. Robert Rose and Rev. Charles Rose
Robert Rose of Connecticut Who Came in 1634
Rose War Files: Vol. I
Rose War Files: Vol. II
Frederick Rose of Virginia, North Carolina
and Tennessee
Andrew Rose of Mercer County, Pennsylvania
Abstracts of Virginia Rose Estates Prior to 1800
Ancestors and Descendants of Anson Parmilee Stone
David Christian Crummey Family
Declarations of Intention Santa Clara County, California 1850-1870

Co-author of

The Complete Idiot's Guide to Genealogy

Foreword

The first publication in 1987 was followed by a second edition in 1995 which included Appendix A and B for Dutch and Frisian Baptismal Names and their English equivalents. In 1998 a new edition added Appendix C, truncated/superscripted names, and Appendix D, names used by both males and females. In 2002 Appendix E, an informative article by the eminent Donald Lines Jacobus Ph.D., FASG, joined the other appendixes. In this present new fifth edition not only are there more nicknames, but also Appendix F listing Italian names with their English equivalents, nicknames, and diminutives.

An understanding of nicknames is crucial in evaluating documents. A common scenario: one record mentions six children. Another list for the same couple also with six children doesn't appear to match because a nickname was not recognized. We are left with a supposed "problem" to solve when an understanding of nicknames could explain the differences. Or, an estate names a wife by one name, but the tombstone shows another. Two wives? Or a nickname?

My hope as always is that this volume will save researchers many hours (and perhaps years) of fruitlessly searching for records for non-existent ancestors who were known by their given names in some records, and nicknames in others.

Christine Rose, CG, CGL, FASG

Introduction

Often, researchers miss records that are indexed under nicknames, especially in states such as Pennsylvania (and others) where the system of subindexing by first name is prevalent. The researcher who examines the "A" subsection of the "J" surnames for Alexander Jones but overlooks the "S" subsection for Sandy Jones may miss important records. An awareness of nicknames is also of major importance in searching soundex census, indexed by first names.

An unfamiliarity with nicknames can also add years to a search. This compiler recalls that as a novice many years ago, almost two years were lost in attempts to find a supposed second marriage for a man whose wife was called "Martha" in one court document, and "Patsy" in another. It was quite a jolt to discover they were the same person; that Patsy was a common nickname for Martha! In another case, considerable time was expended trying to find a "missing" son by the name of Peter before learning that Peter was a common nickname for Patrick, a known son.

Some nicknames are unique to their surname, for instance, many Rhodes are nicknamed "Dusty," many males with surnames starting with Mac or Mc are nicknamed "Mac," etc. The within lists however reflect mostly nicknames for given names.

Some nicknames are common to certain regions, and are unlikely to be found in other parts of the country. In other cases, a common nickname in the 18th and 19th century may have fallen into disuse by the 20th century. Conversely, some present day nicknames were unheard of in earlier years. Another consideration is the nickname used commonly for a particular given name in the earlier times, but used for a different given name in present times. An example is Patsy. Used routinely for Martha in the time of our ancestors, it is now usually used for Patricia.

A few initialed given names are included to alert researchers to common shortening of fuller names. For example, L.G.B. for Little GreenBerry, or L.R. for LeRoy. It should also be noted that any of the nicknames listed can be a given name at birth, rather than a nickname.

A final caution. Don't be hasty in assigning a given name. If the record shows "Willie," is it really William? What about Wilfred or Willard or Willis or Wilmer or Wilton or Wiley, or even a female called Wilhelmina??

C.R.

Female Names - Section One

FOLLOWING NAMES ARE CROSS-INDEXED

Abby	See Abigail
Abigail	Abby, Gail, Nabby
Ada	Adaline
Adaline/ Adeline	Ada, Addy, Dell, Lena
Addy	See Adelaide and Adeline, or any name starting with "Ad"
Adelaide	Addy, Adele, Dell, Della, Heidi
Adele	Addy, Dell, see also Adelaide
Adeline	See Adaline
Adelphia	Adele, Addy, Dell, Delphia, Philly
Agatha	Aggy
Aggy	See Agatha, Agnes, Augusta, or any name starting with "Ag"
Agnes	Aggy, Inez, Nessa, sometimes Nancy
Aileen	Allie, Lena
Alabama	Allie; Bama
Alberta	Allie, Bert, Bertie
Alex	See Alexandra
Alexandra	Alex, Alla, Sandy
Alfreda	Alfy, Freda, Freddy, Frieda
Alfy	See Alfreda
Alice/Alicia	Allie, Elsie, Lisa
Alla	See Alexandra, or any name starting with "Al"
Allie	See Aileen, or any starting with "Al"

Alma	See Almarinda
Almarinda	Alma
Almena	Allie, Mena
Alta	See Altamira
Altamira	Alta; Mira
Amanda	Manda, Mandy
Amelia	Emily, Mel, Millie, see also Parmelia
Ann	Annie, Nan, Nana, Nancy, Nannie/ Nanny, is sometimes a nickname for Antonia /Antoinette, Christiana. Also used for names that are combinations of a first name and Ann, such as Roseanne (Rose Ann), Lucian (Lucy Ann), etc.
Annie	See Ann
Antonia/ Antoinette	Nette, Tony, and sometimes Ann
Ara/Arry	See Arabella, Artilda, or any name starting with "Ar"
Arabella	Ara, Arry, Bella
Arlene	Arly, Lena
Arly	See Arlene
Armeda	Arry, Meda
Armena	Arry, Mena
Armilda	Arry, Milda, Milly
Arminta	Arry, Minta
Arry	See Ara
Artelia	Artie, Telia, Tilly
Artie	See Artelia, or any starting with "Ar"
Artilda	Arry, Tilda
Asenath	Assene, Natty, Sene
Assene	See Asenath
Augusta/ Augustina	Aggy, Gatsy, Gussie, Tina

Bab/Babs	See Barbara
Bama	See Alabama
Barbara	Bab, Babs, Barby, Bobbie
Barby	See Barbara
Bathsheba	Sheba
Bea	See Beatrice
Beady	See Obedience
Beatrice	Bea, Trisha, Trix, Trixie
Becca	See Rebecca
Becky	See Rebecca
Belinda	Belle, Linda
Belle/Bella	See Arabella, Belinda, Isabella, or any name starting with "Bel" or ending with "belle" or "bella"
Bert/Bertie	See Alberta, Bertha, Roberta
Bertha	Birdie, Bert, Bertie
Bess/Bessie	See Elizabeth
Beth/Betsy/ Betty	See Elizabeth (for Beth see also Bethany)
Bethany/ Bethena	Beth, Theny
Biddie/Biddy	See Bridget, Obedience
Birdie	See Bertha
Bobbie	See Barbara, Roberta
Bridey/Bridie	See Bridget
Bridget	Biddie, Biddy, Bridgie, Bridey/Bridie
Bridgie	See Bridget
Brina	See Sabrina
Caledonia	Callie; Dona
Callie	See Caledonia, Calpeurina, Caroline
Calpeurina	Callie; Rina
Camille	Cammie, Cammy, Millie
Cammie/ Cammy	See Camille

Candy	See Candace
Candace	Candy
Carol	See Caroline/Carolyn
Caroline/ Carolyn	Callie, Carol, Carrie, Cassie, Lynn
Carrie	See Caroline/Carolyn
Casey	See K. C.
Cassandra	Cassie, Sandra, Sandy
Cassie	See Caroline/Carolyn, Cassandra, Catherine
Catherine/ Cathleen	Cassie, Cathy, Katie, Kay, Kit, Kittie, Rine, Rina, Trina
Cathy	See Catherine
Cathleen	Same as Catherine, which see
Cecilia	Celia, Cissy
Celia	See Cecilia
Char	See Charlotte
Charlotte	Char, Lotta, Lotty; sometimes Sherry
Clo	See Chloe
Chloe	Clo
Chris/Christy/ Crissy	See Christine/Christiana/Christina
Christine/ Christiana/ Christina	Chris, Crissy, Christy, Tina
Cilla/Cille	See Priscilla, or any name ending with "cilla," "cille," or "cella"
Christiana	Same as Christine, but add Anna
Cinderella	Cindy, Ella
Cindy	See Cinderella, Cynthia, Lucinda
Cissy	Cecilia, or any name with a "sis" sound such as Clarissa, Priscilla, Frances, etc.
Clara	See Clarinda, Clarissa

Clarinda	Clara
Clarissa	Clara; Cissy
Clo	See Chloe
Connie	See Constance
Constance	Connie
Cordelia	Cordy, Delia
Cordessa	Cordy, Essa
Cordy	See Cordelia, Cordessa
Cornelia	Corny, Nelle, Nelly
Corny	See Cornelia
Creasy	See Lucretia
Cynthia	Cindy
Daisy	See Margaret
Darcus	Darkey
Darkey	See Darcus, Dorcus
Darlene	Darry, Lena
Darry	See Darlene
Deb/Debby	See Deborah/Debra
Deborah/ Debra	Deb, Debby
Dee	See Philadelphia
Delia	See Cordelia, Fidelia, or any name ending with "delia"
Delilah	Dell, Della, Lil, Lila, Lillie/Lily
Deliverance	Della, Delly, Dilly, sometimes Experience
Dell/Della	See Adelaide, Adele, Adeline, Adelphia, Delilah, Delores, or any name starting with or containing "del"
Dell/Della	See Delila, Delores
Delores	Dell, Lola, Lolly
Delphia	See Adelphia; sometimes Philadelphia
Desdomona	Mona
Dicey	See Rhodesia; may be others but also used as a given name
Dilly	See Deliverance and Philadelphia

Dina	See Geraldine, or any name ending with "dina" or "dine"
Dolly	See Dorothy
Dona	See Caledonia
Dora	See Isadora, Medora, Theodora, or any name containing "dora"
Dorcus	Darkey; seems to sometimes be interchangeable with Drucie; see Drusilla
Drucie	See Drusilla
Drusilla	Drucie; Ella (see note under Dorcas); Zella
Dorothy	Dolly, Dot, Dotha, Dotty
Dot/Dotha/ Dotty	See Dorothy
Edie/Eddie	See Edith, Edwina
Edith	Eddie; Edie
Edwina	Eddie; Edie
Effie	See Euphemia
Elaine	See Eleanor
Eleanor	Elaine, Ellen, Ellie, Lanna, Lenora, Nelly, Nora
Eliza	See Elizabeth, Louise
Elizabeth	Bess, Bessie, Beth, Betsy, Betty, Eliza, Elspy, Lib, Libby, Lisa, Liza, Liz
Ella/Ellie/ Elly	See Eleanor, Cinderella, Gabriella, Helen, Luella, or any name starting with "El" or ending with "elle" or "ella"
Ellen	See Eleanor, Helen
Elmira	Elly, Mira
Elouise	See Heloise
Elsie	See Alice
Elspy	Elizabeth
Emily	Emmy, Millie; see also Amelia

Em	See Emeline, or any name starting with "Em"
Emeline	Em, Emily, Emma, Emmy, Milly
Emily	See Amelia, Emeline
Emma/Emmy	See Emeline
Erma	See Ermengarde
Ermengarde	Erma
Essa/Essie/ Essy	Any name starting with "Es" or ending with "essa" such as Cordessa, Estelle, Ester, Vanessa, etc.; sometimes used for Euphemia
Estelle	Essy, Stella
Esther	See Hester
Et/Etta/Etty	See Hester, or any name ending with "etta" such as Henrietta, Loretta, Margaretta, etc.
Eugenie	Sometimes Jeannie
Eunice	Nicey
Euphemia	Effie, sometimes Essie
Eustacia	Stacia, Stacy
Experience	sometimes Deliverance
Eve	See Evaline, Genevieve
Eva	See Evaline
Evaline	Eva, Eve, Lena
Faith	Fay
Fanny	See Frances
Fay	See Faith
Felty	See Valentine
Fidelia	Delia
Fina	See Josephine
Flo	See Florence
Flora	See Florence
Florence	Flo, Flora, Floss, Flossie

Floss/Flossie	See Florence
Fran	See Frances
Frances	Cissy, Fanny, Fran, Frankie, Sis
Frankie	See Frances
Freda/Freddy/ Frieda	See Alfreda, Fredericka, Winifred, or any name containing "fred"
Fredericka	Freda, Freddy, Ricka
Frony	See Veronica
Gabby	See Gabriella
Gabrielle/ Gabriella	Ella, Gabby
Gail	See Abigail
Gatsy	Augusta
Genevieve	Eve, Jean, Jenny
Geraldine	Dina, Gerrie, Gerry, Jerry
Gerrie/Gerry	See Geraldine
Gert/Gertie	See Gertrude
Gertrude	Gert, Gertie, Trudy
Gina	Regina, or any name ending with "jean" or "gene"
Gincey	See Jane
Ginger/Ginny	See Virginia
Gretta	See Margretta
Gussie	See Augusta/Augustina
Gwen	See Gwendolyn
Gwendolyn	Gwen, Wendy
Hallie	See Mahala
Hank	See Henrietta
Hannah	Nan, Nannie/Nanny, see also Johannah and Susannah
Harriet	Hat, Hattie
Hat/Hattie	See Harriet
Heidi	Adelaide
Helen(a)	Ella, Ellen, Ellie, Lena

Heloise	Eloise, Lois
Henri	See Henrietta
Henrietta	Etta, Etty, Hank, Henri, Nettie, Retta
Hermione	Hermie
Hepsibah	Hipsie
Hessy	See Hester
Hester	Esther, Et, Etta, Hessy, Hetty
Hetty/Hitty	See Hester, Mehitabel
Humey	See Posthuma
Ib/Ibby	See Isabella
Ina	See Lavina
Inez	See Agnes
Irene	Rena
Isabella	Bella, Belle, Ib, Issy, Nib, Nibby, Tibbie
Isadora	Dora, Issy
Issy	See Isabella, Isadora, or any name starting with "Is"
Jane	Gincey, Janie, Jean, Jennie, Jessie, see also Virginia
Janet	Jessie, see also Jeanette
Janie	See Jane; also Virginia
Jean	See Jane, Jeanette, Virjean; also Genevieve and Virginia
Jeanette	Janet, Jean, Jessie, Nettie
Jeannie	See Jean above; also used sometimes for Eugenie
Jemima	Mima
Jennie	See Genevieve, Jane, Jennifer, Virginia
Jennifer	Jennie
Jerry	See Geraldine
Jessica	Jessie
Jessie	See Jane, Janet, Jeanette, Jessica
Jill	See Julia
Jo	See any name starting with "Jo"

Joan	Nonie, see also Joanna/Johannah
Joanna/ Johannah	Joan, Jody, Hannah
Jody	See Joanna/Johannah
Joey	See Josephine
Josephine	Jo, Joey, Josey, Fina
Josey	See Josephine
Joy	See Joyce
Joyce	Jo, Joy
Juanita	Nettie, Nita
Julie/Julia	Jill
K.C.	Casey (Casey is used for first and middle names starting with K.C., such as Katherine Christine) (Also used for males with double names starting with K.C.)
Karen	See Karenhappuch
Karenhap- puch	Karen
Katherine	Same as Catherine, which see
Kathleen	Same as Catherine, which see
Kay	See Catherine
Keziah	Kizza, Kizzie
Kit/Kittie	See Catherine
Kizza/Kizzie	See Keziah
Lanna	See Eleanor
Lavina/ Lavinia	Ina, Viney
Lee	Any name starting with "Le" or ending with "ley" or containing the "lee" sound
Lena/Lina	See any name ending with "leen," "lina," "lena," "lene" or "line," such as Aileen, Darlene, Cathleen, Magdalena, Philena, etc.

Lenora	Lee, Nora, see also Eleanor
Letha	See Talitha, Tellitha
Letitia	Lettie, Lettice, Titia, Tish
Lettie	See Letitia
Lettice	See Letitia
Lib/Libby	See Elizabeth
Lidia	See Lydia
Lil	See Delilah, Lillian
Lila	See Delilah
Lillian	Lil, Lilly/Lily, Lolly
Lily/Lilly	See Delila, Lillian
Lina	Same as Lena, which see
Linda/Lindy	See Belinda, Malinda, Rosalinda or any name ending with "linda"
Lisa	See Alice, Elizabeth, Melissa
Litha	Talitha
Liv	See Olive/Olivia
Liz/Liza	See Eliza, Elizabeth
Lois	See Heloise, Louise
Lola	See Delores
Lolly	See Delores, Lillian
Loretta	Etta, Lorrie, Retta
Lorraine	Lorrie/Lorry, Raine/Rainey
Lorrie	See Loretta, Lorraine
Lotta/Lotty	See Charlotte
Lou/Lu	See Louise, or any name starting with "Lou" or "Lu"
Louise/Louisa	Eliza, Lois, Lou
Lu	Same as Lou, which see
Lucille	Lu, Cille, Lucy
Lucinda	Cindy, Lu, Lucy
Lucretia	Creasy; Lu
Lucy	See Lucille, Lucinda
Luella	Ella, Lu, Lula
Lula	See Luella, Tullah

Lidia	See Lydia
Lyddy	See Lydia
Lydia	Lidia, Lyddy
Lynn	Any name ending with "lene," "lina," "line," or "lyn," such as Carolyn, Madeline, etc.
Mabel	See Mehitabel
Maddie/ Maddy	See Madeline
Madeline	Lena, Maddie/Maddy, Madge, Magda, Maggie, Maida, Maud
Madge	See Madeline, Margaret
Mae	See Mary
Magda	See Magdelina
Magdalena	Lena, Maggie, sometimes Peggy
Maggie	See Madeline, Magdalena, Margaret/ Margarita
Mahala	Hallie
Maida	See Madeline
Malinda	Linda, Lindy, Mel, Mindy
Mamie	See Mary
Manda/ Mandy	See Amanda, Miranda
Margaret/ Margarita/ Margaretta	Daisy, Gretta, Madge, Maggie, Meg, Midge, Peg, Peggie, Rita; sometimes Margery, Marge
Marge/ Margery	See Margaret
Marietta	Can be Mary Etta, or Mary, or Etta
Martha	Marty, Mat, Mattie, Patsy, Patty
Marty	See Martha
Mary	Mae, Mamie, Mitzi, Molly, Polly
Mat	See Martha

Mate	See Mary
Mattie/Matty	See Martha, Matilda
Matilda	Matty, Maud, Tillie
Matty	See Martha, Matilda
Maud	See Madeline, Matilda
Meda	See Armeda
Medora	Dora
Meg	See Margaret
Mehitabel	Hetty, Hitty, Mabel, Mitty
Mel	See Amelia, Melinda, Melissa, Pamela, or any name starting with Mel or containing "mel"
Melia	See Parmelia
Melissa	Lisa, Mel, Milly, Missy, see also Millicent
Mena	See Almena, Armena
Michelle	Mickey
Mickey	See Michelle
Midge	See Margaret
Milda	See Armilda
Mildred	Milly
Millicent	Milly, Missy
Millie/Milly	See Amelia, Armilda, Camille, Emeline, Emily, Mildred, Melissa, Millicent, Parmelia, or any name with "mil" or "mel"
Mimi	See Miriam
Mina	See Wilhelmina
Mindy	See Melinda
Minerva	Minnie; Nerva
Minnie	See Minerva, Wilhelmina
Minta	See Arminta
Mira	See Elmira
Miranda	Mandy, Mira, Randy
Miriam	Mimi, Mitzi

Missy	See Melissa, Millicent
Mitty	See Mehitabel, Submit
Mitzie	See Mary, Miriam
Molly	See Mary
Mona	See Desdomona
Myra	See Altamira; Elmira
Nabby	See Abigail
Nan/Nana	See Ann, Nancy, Hannah
Nancy	Nan, Nannie (Nancy also used as nickname for Ann, and sometimes for Agnes)
Nannie/ Nanny	See Ann, Nancy, Hannah
Naomi	Oma
Nappy	See Penelope
Natalie	Natty, Nettie
Natty	See Asenath, Natalie
Neecy	See Pernecia
Nell/Nelle/ Nelly	See Cornelia, Eleanor, Prunella
Nerva	See Minerva
Nessa	See Agnes, or any name with "ess" or name ending with "essa" such as Vanessa
Netta/Nette/ Nettie	See Antoinette, Henrietta, Jeanette, Juanita, Natalie, and all names ending with "netta," "nette," "nita"
Nib/Nibby	See Isabella
Nicole	Nikky
Nicey	See Eunice
Nikky	See Nicole
Nita	Juanita
Nolly	See Olivia
Nora	See Eleanor, Lenora

Obed	See Obedience
Obedience	Beady, Biddie, Obed
Olive/Olivia	Liv, Olly, Nolly
Olly	See Olivia; sometimes for Polly
Oma	See Naomi
Pam	See Pamela
Pamela	Mel, Pam
Parmelia	Amelia, Melia, Milly
Pat	See Patricia, Patience, see also Patsy/Patty
Patience	Pat, Patty
Patricia	Pat, Patsy, Patty, Tricia
Patsy/Patty	See Martha, especially in older records; now usually for Patricia
Patty	See Patsy; sometimes also for Patience; now usually for Patricia
Paula	Polly, see also Paulina
Paulina	Lina, Polly
Peg/Peggie	See Margaret
Penelope	Nappy, Penny
Penny	See Penelope
Pernecia	Neecy
Phena	See Tryphena
Philadelphia	Dee, Delphia, Dilly, Philly
Philena	Lena; Philly
Philly	See Adelphia, Philadelphia; Philena
Polly	See Mary, Olly, Paula, Paulina
Posthuma	Humey
Priscilla	Cissy, Cilla, Prissy
Prissy	See Priscilla
Prudence	Prudy, Prue
Prudy	See Prudence
Prue	See Prudence; Prunella
Prunella	Nellie, Prue
Rachel	Shelly

Raine/Rainey	See Lorraine
Randy	See Miranda
Reba	See Rebecca
Rebecca	Becca, Becky, Reba
Reggie	See Regina
Regina	Gina, Reggie
Rena/Rina	See Catherine, Irene, Serena, or any ending with "rene," "rine," or "rena"
Retta	See Henrietta, Loretta, or any name ending with "retta"
Rhodesia	Dicey, Roddy
Ricka	See Fredericka
Rina	Same as Rena, which see
Rita	See Margaret/Margarita
Robbie	See Roberta
Roberta	Bert, Bobbie, Robbie
Roddy	See Rhodesia
Ron/Rona/ Ronnie	See Veronica
Rosabel	Belle, Rosa, Rose, Roz
Rosa/Rose	See any name starting with "Rosa" or "Rose" or ending with "rosa" or "rose"
Rosalyn/ Rosalinda	Linda, Rosa, Rose, Roz
Roseann	Ann, Rose, Roz
Roxanne	Ann, Rose, Roxy
Roxy	See Roxanne
Roz	See any name starting with "Ros"
Sabrina	Brina
Sadie	See Sarah
Sammie/ Sammy	See Samantha
Samantha	Sammie/Sammy
Sandra/ Sandy	See Alexandra, Cassandra

Sal/Sally	See Sarah, sometimes Selina
Sarah	Sadie, Sal, Sally
Savannah	Van, Vanna
Selina	Lena, sometimes Sally
Sene	See Asenath
Serena	Rina
Sheba	See Bathsheba
Shelly	See Rachel
Sherry	Shirley; sometimes Charlotte
Shirley	Lee, Sherry, Shirl
Sis/Sissy	Same as Cissy, which see
Sookey	See Susan/Susannah
Stacia/Stacy	See Eustacia
Stella	See Estelle
Submit	Mitty
Sukey	See Susan/Susannah
Susan/ Susannah	Hannah, Sookey, Sue, Sukey, Susie
Tabitha	Tabby; sometimes seems to be interchangeable with Dorcas
Talitha	Letha, Litha, Telia
Tanky	Thankful
Teddi/Teddy	See Theodora
Telia	See Artelia, Talitha, Tellitha
Tellitha	Letha, Telia
Tempy	See Temperance
Temperance	Tempy
Tess/Tessie	See Theresa
Thankful	Tanky
Theda	See Theodora
Theny	See Bethany, Bethena
Theo	See Theodora
Theodora	Dora, Teddi, Theda, Theo
Theresa	Terry, Tess, Tessie, Thirza, Thursa, Tracy

Thirza	See Theresa
Thursa	See Theresa
Tibbie	See Isabella
Tilly	See Matilda
Tina	Any name ending in "tine" or "tina," such as Augustina, Christine, Valentine, etc.
Tish/Titia	See Letitia
Tony	See Antonia/Antoinette
Tracy	See Theresa
Trina	See Catherine
Tricia/Trisha/ Trix/Trixie	See Beatrice, Patricia
Trudy	See Gertrude
Tullah	Lula
Tryphena	Phena
Val	See Valentine
Valentine	Felty, Tina, Val
Van/Vanna	See Savannah, Vanessa
Vanessa	Essa, Nessa, Van, Vanna
Veronica	Franky, Frony, Ron, Ronna, Ronnie, Vonnie
Vicki	See Victoria
Victoria	Vicki
Viney	See Lavinia
Virjean	Jean, Virgy
Virginia	Ginger, Ginny, Jane, Jennie, Virgy
Virgy	See Virginia, VirJean
Vonnie	See Veronica
Wendy	See Gwendolyn
Wilhelmina	Mina, Willie, Wilma, Minnie
Willie	See Wilhelmina
Wilma	See Wilhelmina
Winifred	Freddie, Winnie, Winnet
Winnet	See Winifred

Winnie	See Winifred
Zella/Zilla	See Barzilla, Drucilla, Zerilda, and any name ending with "zilla" or "zella"
Zerilda	Zilla
Zilla	See Zella

Male Names - Section Two

A.B.	See Abijah
Aaron	Erin, Ron, Ronnie
Ab	Any name starting with "Ab"
Abe	See Abraham/Abram
Abel	Ab, Abe, Eb, Ebbie
Abiah/ Abijah	A.B., Ab, Biah
Abiel	Ab, Bial, Biel
Abraham/ Abram	Abe
Abner	Ab
Ad/Ade	Any name starting with "Ad"
Adam	Ad, Ade
Adelbert	Ad, Ade, Albert, Bert, Del, Delbert, Elbert
Adolph/ Adolphus	Ad, Dolph, Olph
Al	Any name starting with "Al"
Alan	Al, see also Alanson
Alanson	Al, Alan, Lonson
Albert	Al, Bert, Elbert, see also Adelbert
Aldrich	Al, Rich, Richie
Alex	See Alexander
Alexander	Al, Alex, Eleck, Sandy, Zandy
Alfred	Al, Fred
Alonzo	Al, Lon, Lonzo
Ander	See Anderson
Anderson	Ander, Andy, Sonny
Andrew	Andy, Drew
Andy	See Anderson, Andrew
Ang/Angie	Angelo

Angelo	Ang, Angie
Anthony	Tony
Archibald/ Archibaldo	Archie, Baldo
Archie	See Archibald
Art	See Arthur
Arthur	Art
Auggie	See August
August	Auggie
Azariah	Aze, Riah
Aze	See Azariah
Auggie	See August, Augustine, Augustus
August	See Augustine/Augustus, or, used by itself as a given name. Auggie some times used as a nickname
Augustine/ Augustus	August, Austin, Gus
Austin	See Augustine/Augustus
B. F.	Often for Benjamin Franklin
Baldo	See Archibald
Barnabas	Barney, Berney
Barney	See Barnabus, Bernard
Bart/Bartel/Bat	See Bartholomew
Bartholomew	Bart, Bartel, Bat, Mees, Meus
Bass	See Sebastian
Bela/Bele	sometimes used for William
Ben	Any name starting with "Ben" such as Benajah, Benjamin, Bennett, Bentley, Benton, etc.
Benedict	Ben, Bennie; sometimes Bennett
Benjamin	Ben, Benjy, Bennie, Jamie
Benjy	See Benjamin
Bennett	Ben, Bennie; see also Benedict
Bennie	See Benjamin, Bennett
Bernard	Barney, Berney

Berney	See Barnabus, Bernard
Berry	See Greenberry, Littleberry or any name ending with "berry"
Bert	Any name starting or ending with "bert" such as Albert, Bertram, Delbert, Filbert, Gilbert, Hubert, etc.
Biah	See Abiah/Abijah
Bial/Biel	See Abiel
Bias	See Tobias
Bill/Billy	See William
Bob/Bobby	See Robert
Bonaparte	Bony
Bony	Bonaparte
Brad	See Bradford
Bradford	Brad, Brady, Ford
Brady	See Bradford, Broderick
Broderick	Brady, Brody, Ricky
Brody	See Broderick
Bron	See Bronson
Bronson	Bron, Sonny
Bud	A common nickname for Junior, but can be for any name
Cal	See Calvin
Calvin	Cal, Vin, Vinny
Cam	See Cameron
Cameron	Cam, Ron, Ronny
Carl	See Charles
Casey	See K. C.
Ced	See Cedric
Cene	See Cyrenius
Cedric	Ced, Rick
Chan	Chauncey
Charles	Carl, Charlie, Chick, Chuck
Charlie	See Charles
Chauncey	Chan

Ches/Chess	See Chester
Chester	Ches, Chess, Chet
Chet	See Chester
Chick	See Charles
Chris	See Christian/Christopher
Christian/ Christopher	Chris, Kit
Chuck	See Charles
Chy	Zachary
Claas	See Nicholas
Claiborne	Clay
Clair/Clare	See Clarence
Clarence	Clair, Clare
Clay	See Claiborne
Clem	See Clement
Clement	Clem
Cliff	See Clifford, Clifton, or any name starting with "Clif"
Clifford	Cliff, Ford
Clifton	Cliff, Tony
Clum	See Columbus
Cole	Any name starting with "Col" such as Colby, Coleman, etc.
Columbus	Clum, Lum
Con/Conny	See Cornelius, or any name starting with "Con" such as Conrad, Conant
Conrad	Con, Conny
Cornelius	Con, Conny, Corny, Neil
Corny	See Cornelius
Court	See Courtney
Courtney	Court, Curt
Crawford	Ford
Cyrenius	Cene, Cy, Renius, Serene, Swene
Curt	See Courtney, Curtis
Curtis	Curt

Cy	Any name starting with "Cy" such as Cyrenius, Cyril, Cyrus etc.
Dahl/Dal	See Dalton
Dalton	Dahl, Dal, Tony
Dan/Danny	See Daniel and Sheridan or any name starting or ending with "dan"
Daniel	Dan, Danny
David	Dave, Davy, Day
Dave/Davy	See David
Day	See David
Dee	See Zebedee, sometimes for names starting with "De"
Del	See Adelbert, Delbert or any name containing "del"
Delbert	Bert, Del
Delineaus	Lineau
Dennis	See Dennison
Dennison	Dennis, Denny
Denny	See Dennison
Derrick	Eric, Rick, Ricky
Diah	Any name ending with "diah" such as Jedediah, Obadiah, Zedediah, etc.
Dick	See Dietrick, Richard
Dicken	See Richard
Dietrick	Dick
Dite/Ditus	Epaphroditus
Dob/Dobbin	See Robert
Dolph	See Adolph/Adolphus, Randolph, Rudolph/Rudolphus or any name containing "dolph"
Dom	See Dominick
Dominick	Dom, Nick
Don	See Donald
Donald	Don, Donnie
Donnie	See Donald

Drew	See Andrew, Woodrow
Duke	Marmaduke
Dunk	See Humphrey
Dyce/Cyche	Epaphroditus
Dyer	Same as Diah, which see
Eb/ Ebbie	See Abel, or any starting with "Eb"
Eben	See Ebenezer
Ebenezer	Eb, Ebbie, Eben
Ed	See Edmund, Edward, Edwin, or any name starting with "Ed"
Edmund	Ed, Ned, Ted
Edward	Ed, Ned, Ted
Edwin	Ed, Ned, Winny
Elbert	See Adelbert, Albert
Eleazer	Lazar
Eleck	See Alexander
Eli	Any name starting with "Eli"
Elias	Eli, Lee, Lias
Elijah	Eli, Lige
Eliphalet	Left
Elisha	Eli, Lish
Elwood	Woody
Emanuel	Manny, Manuel
Eph	See Ephraim
Ephraim	Eph
Epaphroditus	Dite, Ditus, Dyce, Dyche, Eppa
Eppa	See Epaphroditus
Eric	Rick, Ricky; also nickname for names containing an "eric" sound such as "Derrick"
Erin	See Aaron
Ernest	Ernie
Ernie	See Ernest
Erskine	Kinny
Esquire	Squire

Eugene	Gene
Ez	Any name starting with "Ez" such as Ezekiel, Ezra, etc.
Ezekiel	Ez, Zeke
Ezra	Ez
Fate	See Lafayette
Field	Any name ending with "field" such as Garfield, Winfield etc.
Ferdie	See Ferdinand
Ferdinand	Ferdie, Fernando
Fernando	See Ferdinand
Filbert	Bert, Phil
Fitz	Names starting with or containing "fitz" such as Fitzgerald
Ford	Any name ending with "ford" such as Bradford, Clifford, Crawford, etc.
Fran	See Francis, Franklin
Frank	See Francis, Franklin
Francis	Fran, Frank
Franklin	Fran, Frank
Fred/Freddie/ Freddy	See Alfred and Frederick, also names ending with "fred" such as Wilfred
Frederick	Fred, Freddie, Fritz
Fritz	See Frederick
G.B.	Often Greenberry
G.W.	Often George Washington
Gabby	See Gabriel
Gabe	See Gabriel
Gabriel	Gabby, Gabe
Gaistone	Gus
Garfield	Field, Gar
Garvin	Gar, Vin, Vinny
Gene	See Eugene
Geoff	See Geoffrey/Jeffrey

Geoffrey/ Jeffrey	Geoff, Jeff
Gerald	Gerry, Jerry
Gerry	See Gerald
Gil	See Gilbert, or any name starting with "Gil" such as Gilman
Gilbert	Bert, Gil, Wilber
Greenberry	Berry, Green, frequently G.B.
Gum	See Montgomery
Gus	See Augustine/Augustus, Gustane, Gustavus or any name starting with or containing "gus"
Gustane/ Gustine/ Guston	Gus (Gustane etc. can also be used as a nickname for Augustine, and occasionally for Augustus)
Gustavus	Gus
Hal	See Henry, Harold, or any names starting with "Hal" such as Halsey
Halsey	Hal
Hank	See Henry
Harold	Hal, Harry
Harry	See Harold, Henry
Henry	Hal, Hank, Harry
Herb	See Herbert
Herbert	Bert, Herb
Hez	See Hezekiah, Hiram
Hezekiah	Hez, Hy, Kiah
Hiel	See Jehiel
Hiram	Hez, Hy
Hob/Hobkin	See Robert
Hodge	See Roger/Rodger
Horace	Horry
Horry	See Horace

Hubert	Hub, Hugh, Bert
Hugh	Sometimes for Hubert
Humph	See Humphrey
Humphrey	Dunk; Humph
Hy	See Hezekiah, Hiram
Iggy	See Ignatius
Ignatius	Iggy, Nace, Nate, Natius
Ike	See Isaac
Isaac	Ike, Zeke
Isidore	Izzy
Izzy	See Isidore
Jaap	See Jacob
Jack	See John; sometimes for Jacques
Jacob	Jaap, Jake, Jay. Sometimes shortened from Jacobus (Dutch) though Jacobus translates to James
Jacques	Sometimes Jack
Jake	See Jacob
James	Jamie, Jem, Jim, Jimmy [see also Jacob]
Jamie	See Benjamin, James
Jay	See Jacob
Jed	See Jedediah
Jedediah	Diah, Dyer, Jed
Jeff	Any name starting with "Jeff" such as Jefferson and Jeffrey
Jefferson	Jeff, Sonny
Jeffrey/ Geoffrey	Jeff
Jehiel	Hiel
Jem	See James
Jereme	See Jeremiah
Jeremiah	Jereme, Jerry
Jerry	See Gerald, Jeremiah or any name starting with "Ger" or "Jer"

Jim/Jimmy	See James
Jock	See John
Joe/Joey	Joseph
John	Jack, Jock, Johnny (John can also occasionally be used as a nickname for Jonathan)
Johnny	See John
Jonathan	Nathan; sometimes John
Jos	Any name starting with "Jos" such as Joseph, Joshua, Josiah, etc.
Joseph	Joe, Joey, Jos
Josh	Joshua
Joshua	Jos, Josh
Josiah	Jos
Jud	See Judson; sometimes used for Judge
Judson	Jud, Sonny
Jule	Julian, Julius, or any name starting with "Jul"
Julian	Jule
Julius	Jule
K.C.	Casey (Casey or K.C. is used for first and middle names starting with K.C., such as Kenneth Christopher.) (Note that it can also be used for female double names.)
Ken/Kenny	Any name starting with "Ken" such as Kendall, Kendrick, Kenneth, Kent, etc. Also names ending with "kin" or "kine" such as Erskine
Kiah	See Hezekiah
Kit	See Christian/Christopher
King	Any name starting with King, such as Kingston, Kingsley, etc.
Kinny	Same as Kenny, which see
L.B.	Sometimes Littleberry

L.G.B.	Often Little Greenberry
L.R.	Sometimes LeRoy
Lafayette	Fate
Lamont	Monty
Lance	See Lancelot
Lancelot	Lance, Lot
Lanny	See Orlando and Roland
Larry	See Lawrence
Lazar	See Eleazer
Lawrence	Larry, Lon, Lorne, Lorry
Left	See Eliphalet
Lem	See Lemuel
Lemuel	Lem
Lee	Any name with a "lee" sound such as LeRoy, Leland, etc.; also Elias
Leet	See Philetus
Len/Lenny	See Leonard
Leo	See Leonard, Leopold
Leon	See Leonard and Napoleon or any name containing "leon"
Leonard	Leo, Leon, Len, Lenny, Lineau
Leopold	Leo
LeRoy	Lee, Roy
Les	See Leslie,Lester,or any name starting with "Les"
Leslie	Les
Lester	Les
Lias	See Elias
Lige	See Elijah
Lincoln	Link
Lindy	See Lyndon
Lineau	See Delineaus and Leonard
Link	See Lincoln
Lish	See Elisha
Littleberry	Berry, Little, often L.B.

Little Greenberry	Often L.G.B.
Lon	See Alonzo, Lawrence, Napoleon, or any name ending in "Lon"
Lonzo	See Alonzo
Lorne	See Lawrence
Lonson	See Alanson/Alansing
Lorry	See Lawrence
Lot	See Lancelot
Lou/Louie	See Louis
Louis	Lou, Louie, Ludwig/Ludwick
Lucias/Lucas	Luke
Ludwig/Ludwick	See Louis
Luke	See Lucias/Lucas, Luther
Luther	Luke
Lum	See Columbus
Lyndon	Lindy, Lynn
Lynn	See Lyndon
Mal	Any name starting with "Mal" such as Malcolm
Manny/Manuel	See Emanuel
Marcus	Mark
Marcus Dee	See Marques DeLafayette
Mark	See Marcus
Marmaduke	Duke
Marques DeLafayette	Marcus Dee
Martin	Marty
Marty	See Martin
Marv	See Mervyn/Marvin
Matt	See Matthew/Matthias
Matthew/Matthias	Matt, Thias, Thys

Maurice/ Morris	Morey
Max	Any name starting with "Max," such as Maxmillan, Maxwell, etc.
Mees/Meus	See Bartholomew
Merv	See Mervyn/Marvin
Mervyn/ Marvin	Merv, Marv
Micah	Sometimes for Michael
Mike	See Michael
Michael	Mickey, Mike; sometimes Micah
Mickey	See Michael
Mitch	See Mitchell
Mitchell	Mitch
Montgomery	Gum, Monty
Monty	Any name containing "mont," such as Montgomery, Lamont, etc.
Morey	See Maurice/Morris, Seymour
Mos	See Moses
Moses	Mos, Moze
Moze	See Moses
Nace	See Ignatius
Naldo	See Reginald, Ronald
Nap	See Napoleon
Napoleon	Nap, Nappy, Leon
Nappy	See Napoleon
Nat	See Nathaniel
Nate	See Ignatius, Nathaniel
Nathan	Nate; see also Jonathan
Nathaniel	Nat, Nate, Natty, Than; sometimes shortened to Nathan
Natius	See Ignatius
Natty	See Nathaniel
Ned	See Edmund, Edward, or any name starting with "Ed"

Neil	See Cornelius
Nicholas	Claas, Claes, Nick
Nick/Nicky	See Dominick, Nicholas, or any name starting or ending with "nick"
Norbert	Bert, Norby
Norby	See Norbert
Obadiah	Diah, Dyer, Obed, Obie
Obed/Obie	See Obadiah
Oliver	Ollie
Ollie	See Oliver
Orlan	See Orlando
Olph	See Adolphus, Rudolphus, Theophilus
Oph	Theophilus
Orlando	Lanny, Orlan; also variant of Roland
Oswald	Ossy, Ozzy, Waldo
Ossy/Ozzy	Any name starting with "Os" such as Oscar, Osmond, Oswald, etc.
Paddy	See Patrick
Pat	Any name starting with "Pat" such as Patrick, Patterson, etc.
Pate	See Peter, Patrick
Patrick	Paddy, Pat, Patsy, Peter. Sometimes Pate
Patsy	See Patrick
Pelegrine	Perry G.
Percivial	Percy
Percy	Sometimes for Percival
Perry G.	See Pelegrine
Peter	Pete, sometimes Pate. See also Patrick
Phil	See Filbert, or any name starting with "Phil"
Philetus	Leet, Phil
Philip	Phil
Pres	See Prescott
Prescott	Pres, Scott, Scotty

Rafe	See Raphael
Ralph	Sometimes for Raphael
Rance	See Ransome
Randolph	Dolph, Randy
Randy	Any name starting with "Ran" such as Randall, Randolph, Ransome, etc.
Ransome	Rance, Randy
Raphael	Rafe, Ralph
Ray	See Raymond
Raymond	Ray
Reg/Reggie	See Reginald
Reginald/ Reginaldo	Naldo, Reg, Reggie, Renny
Renius	See Cyrenius
Renny	See Reginald
Reuben	Rube
Riah	Any name ending with "riah" such as Azariah, Uriah
Rial	See Uriah
Rich/Richie	See Aldrich, Richard
Richard	Dick, Dicken, Rich, Rick, Ricky
Rick/Ricky	See Eric and any name starting with "Rich" or ending with "ric" or "rick" such as Broderick, Cedric, Frederick, Theodrick, etc.
Riley	See Uriah
Riverus	Verus
Rob/Robbie	See Robert
Robert	Bob, Bobbie, Dob, Dobbin, Hob, Hobkin, Rob, Robbie, Robin, Rupert
Robin	See Robert; also used for Robinson
Rod	Any name starting with "Rod" such as Roderick, Rodger, Rodney, etc.
Rog	See Roger/Rodger
Roger/Rodger	Hodge, Rod, Rog

Rollo/Rolly	See Roland
Roland	Lanny, Rollo, Rolly; also variant for Orlando
Ron	See Aaron, also any names starting with "Ron," or ending with "ron" such as Cameron, Ronald, etc.
Ronald	Ron, Naldo
Ronny	Same as Ron, which see
Roy	See LeRoy, also any containing "Roy"
Rube	See Reuben
Rudolph/ Rudolphus	Dolph, Olph, Rolf, Rudy
Rudy	Any name starting with "Rud" such as Rudolph, Rudyard, etc.
Rupert	See Robert
Russ	See Russell
Russell	Russ, Rusty
Rusty	See Russell
Ryal	See Uriah
Sal/Salmon	See Solomon
Sam/Sammy	See Samuel
Samuel	Sam, Sammy
Sandy	See Alexander
Saul	See Solomon
Sebastian	Bass
See	See Seymour
Serene	See Cyrenius
Seymour	Morey, See
Scott/Scotty	Prescott or any containing "scott"
Shel/ Shelly	Any name starting with "Shel" such as Shelby, Shelton, etc.
Shelton	Shel, Shelly, Tony
Sher	See Sheridan
Sheridan	Dan, Danny, Sher
Si	See Sylvester, or names starting with "Si"

Sid	See Sidney
Sidney	Sid, Syd
Silas	Sy
Simon/ Simeon	Si, Sion
Sion	See Simon/Simeon
Sly	See Sylvester
Smith	Smitty
Smitty	See Smith
Sol/Solly	See Solomon
Solomon	Sal, Salmon, Saul, Sol, Solly, Zolly
Sonny	See Anderson, Bronson, Judson, or any name ending with "son"
Squire	See Esquire
Stan	Any name starting with "Stan" such as Stanford, Stanley, etc.
Staves	See Gustavus
Steene	See Stephen
Steph	See Stephen/Steven
Stephen/ Steven	Steene, Steph, Steve
Sullivan	Sully, Van
Sully	See Sullivan
Swene	See Cyrenius
Sy	See Silas, or any name starting with "Si" and "Sy" such as Sylvester
Syd	See Sidney
Syl	See Sylvanus, Sylvester
Sylvanus	Syl, Van
Sylvester	Si, Sly, Sy, Syl, Vess, Vester, Vet
Tad	See Thaddeus
Ted	See Edmund, Edward and Theodore, or any names starting with "Ed" and "Ted"
Terence	Terry
Terry	See Terence

Thad	See Thaddeus
Thaddeus	Tad, Thad
Than	See Nathaniel
Theo	Theodore, Theodrick, Theophilus
Theodore	Ted, Teddy, Theo
Theodrick	Rick, Theo
Theophilus	Olph, Oph, Theo
Thias	See Matthew/Matthias
Thomas	Tom, Tommy
Thornton	Thorny
Thorny	See Thornton
Thys	See Mathew/Matthias
Tim/Timmy	See Timothy
Timothy	Tim, Timmy
Tobias	Bias, Toby
Toby	See Tobias
Tom/Tommy	See Thomas
Tony	See Anthony, also any name ending with "ton" such as Clifton, Dalton, Shelton, etc.
Ty	Any name starting with "Ty" such as Tyler, Tyrone, etc.
Uriah	Riah, Rial, Riley, Ryal
Val	See Valentine
Valentine	Val (also used as a name for females)
Van	Sylvanus, also any name ending with "van" such as Sullivan; also used for surnames starting with "Van"
Verus	See Riverus
Vess	See Sylvester
Vester	See Sylvester
Vet	See Sylvester
Vin/Vince	See Calvin, Garvin, Vincent/Vinson, or any name starting or ending with "vin"

Vincent/ Vinson	Vin, Vince, Vinny
Vinny	Same as Vin, which see
Waldo	See Oswald
Wallace	Wally
Wally	See Wallace
Walter	Walt, Watt
Wash	Washington (often George Washington)
Washington	Wash
Watt	See Walter
Wilber	See Gilbert
Wilfred	Fred, Will, Willie
Will/Willie	Any name starting with "Wil" such as Wilfred, Willard, William, etc.
William	Bill, Billy, Will, Willie; sometimes Bele, Bela
Win	See Edwin, or any name starting with "Win" such as Winfield
Winfield	Field, Win, Winny
Winny	Same as Win, which see
Woodrow	Drew, Woody
Woody	Any name containing "wood" such as Elwood, Woodrow, etc.
Zach	See Zachariah
Zachariah	Zach, Zachy, Zeke
Zachary	Chy
Zandy	See Alexander
Zeb	See Zebedee
Zebedee	Dee, Zeb
Zedediah	Diah, Dyer, Zed
Zed	See Zedediah
Zeke	See Ezekiel, Isaac, Zachariah
Zeph	See Zephaniah
Zephaniah	Zeph
Zolly	See Solomon

Appendix A

Dutch and Frisian Baptismal Names and Their Equivalents in English

This listing is mostly from Gustave Anjou, Ph.D., Ulster County, N.Y. *Probate Records in the office of the surrogate [etc.]* ... (New York: Gustave Anjou, 1906), Vol. I. See Appendix B for English to Dutch/Frisian.

Dutch/Frisian	English
Aaghie	Agatha
Aagje	Agatha
Aagt	Agatha
Aaltje	Alice
Aart	Arthur
Adda	Alice
Adelheyd	Adelaide
Adriance	Adrienne
Adriaantje	Adrian
Aefje	Eva
Aeltje	Alice
Aert	Arthur
Aetje	Eve
Agnietje	Agnes
Agt	Agatha
Alberick	Alberic
Aldert	Albert
Alerta	Alice
Alewijn	Alwin
Alyd	Adelaide
Alta	Alida
Annatje	Anne
Andreas	Andrew
Andries	Andrew
Anghe	Agnes
Angeniete	Agnes
Annechet	Anne
Anneken	Anne
Annetje	Anne
Antie	Anne
Antje	Anne
Arendt	Arnold
Ariaan	Adrian
Arie	Adrian
Arriaantje	Adrian
Augustijn	Austen
Badeloch	Beatrice
Balt	Balthazar
Baltje	Balthazar
Baltrus	Balthazar
Barber	Barbara
Barend	Bernard
Barent	Barent
Bart	Bartholomew
Bartel	Bartholomew
Bartelmus	Bartholomew
Bartje	Barbara
Bastian	Sebastian

Dutch/Frisian	English
Batje	Bathilde
Beeltje	Neeltje, Cornelia
Beletje	Arabella
Bell	Isabella
Bella	Isabella
Bernd	Bernard
Bert	Gilbert
Bertus	Albertus
Beth	Elizabeth
Betje	Elizabeth
Blaas	Blasius
Boudje	Balldwin
Boldwijn	Baldwin
Bonifaas	Boniface
Boudewyn	Baldwin
Bram	Abraham
Bregje	Bridget
Carel	Charles
Case	Cornelius
Casper	Jasper
Catrijn	Catharine
Ceerles	Charles
Celia	Cecilia
Cheerelz	Charles
Cheiltje	Cornelia
Chime	James
Christoffel	Christopher
Christyntje	Christina
Classje	Clasine
Claes	Nicholas
Coen	Conrd
Coenraad	Conrad
Coenraadt	Conrad
Cornelis	Cornelius
Crispijn	Crispin
Daaf	David
Daam	Adam
Daatje	Alice
Denys	Dionysius
Deerick	Theodoric
Desin	Gerardina
Dierderick	Theodoric
Dientje	Bernardina
Diewertje	Debora
Dina	Bernardina
Dirk	Theodoric
Dirkje	Theodoric
Dolf	Adolphus
Door	Dorothy
Doortje	Dorothy
Doostie	Theodosia
Dort	Dorothy
Dortchen	Dora
Dorus	Theodore
Dries	Andrew
Eefje	Eve
Eelet	Helena
Eike	Agnes
Els	Aletta
Elsje	Aletta
Emmetje	Emily
En	Anne
Engel	Angelica
Engelina	Angelica
Engeltje	Angelica
Enrik	Henry
Epje	Egbert
Ethilrede	Awdry
Evert	Everard
Eyntje	Annie
Eytic	Ida
Femmetje	Frances, Fanny
Fick	Sophia
Fletje	Sophia
Floortje	Florentina
Florentijntje	Florentina
Floris	Florian
Francijntje	Frances, Fanny
Francina	Fanny
Frans	Francis

Dutch/Frisian	English	Dutch/Frisian	English
Fransje	Frances, Fanny	Heintje	Henry
Freek	Frederick	Hendrica	Henriette
Frem	Ephraim	Hendrikje	Henriette
Frerk	Frederick	Hentje	Henriette
Friko	Frederick	Heyltje	Helena
Frits	Frederic	Hieronimus	Jerome
Fytje	Sophia	Hilligond	Hilda
Garret	Gerard	Hilletje	Hilda
Geertje	Gertrude	Hiskia	Hezekiah
Geert	Gerard	Huigen	Hugo
Geertie	Gertrude	Huybert	Hubert
Geertje	Gertrude	Ifje	Eve
Geertrui	Gertrude	Ikee	Agnes
Geertruida	Gertrude	Jaantje	Jane
Geertruyd	Gertrude	Jaap	Jacob
Geesje	Gerarda	Jaapie	Jacob
Geleyn	Giles	Jacob	James
Gellis	Giles	Jacoba	Jacobina
Gepje	Rachel	Jacobje	Jacob
Gerrit	Gerard	Jacobus	James
Gerritje	Geraldina	Jacomyntje	Jemima
Giel	Michael	Jaepje	Jacob
Gijs	Gilbert	Jan	John
Gijsbertus	Gilbert	Janneken	Jane
Godfried	Godfrey	Jannetje	Jane
Goris	George	Janotje	Jane
Goverd	Godfrey, Timothy	Jansje	Jane
		Jantina	Jane
Griet	Margaret, Madge, Peg	Jantje	Johnny
		Japic	Jacob
Grietje	Meg, Peggy	Jeremias	Jeremiah
Guido	Guy	Jeronimus	Jerome
Gysbert	Gilbert	Jetje	Henriette
Gyslbert	Gilbert	Joannes	John
Hannes	John, Jackie	Joaptie	Jacob
Hans	John, Jack	Jobje	Jacob
Hansje	Joan, Johanna	Jochem	Joachim
Harck	Hercules	Johannes	John
Harmen	Herman	Joost	Justin, Joseph
Hein	Henry	Joris	George

Dutch/Frisian	English
Josyntje	Josine
Juliaantje	Juliana
Jurgen	George
Jurian	George
Jurn	George
Jurrian	George
Jury	George
Justin	Justin
Justje	Jenny
Kaat	Catharine
Kaatje	Kate, Kitty
Karel	Charles
Kareltje	Charles
Katrijn	Catharine
Katryntje	Kate, Kathleen
Kee	Cornelia
Kees	Cornelius
Keesje	Cornelius
Keetje	Cornelia
Kersten	Christian
Kesia	Kathleen
Klaar	Clare
Klaartje	Clare
Klaas	Nicholas
Klaasje	Nicholas, Nick
Krelis	Cornelius
Ko	James, Jemmy, Jem
Koba	Jacobus Koba
Koosje	Jacobina
Koris	Cornelius
Korsten	Christian
Krelius	Cornelius
Kris	Christian
Krischan	Christian
Krisje	Christina
Kristel	Christina
Kristijntje	Christina
Kruschen	Christian
Kyrn	Quirine
Lambrecht	Lambert
Laurens	Lawrence
Leen	Leonard
Leendert	Leonard
Leentje	Magdalena
Lena	Magdalena
Lenoor	Eleanoor
Letje	Adeline
Lezart	Elise
Lieve	Leo
Lijsbert	Lisbet
Lijsje	Lise
Lodewijk	Lewis
Lotje	Charlotte
Loures	Lewis
Louw	Lawrence
Lucia	Lucy
Ludovicus	Louis
Lukas	Luke
Luytje	Luke
Lys	Lisbet
Lysbet	Lisbet
Lysje	Lise
Maaicke	Mary
Maarten	Martin
Maartje	Martina
Maas	Bartholomew
Machiel	Michael
Machteld	Mathilda
Magdaleentje	Magdalen
Magtelt	Mathilda
Manus	Herman
Margit	Margaret
Margriet	Margaret
Margrietje	Margaret
Marij	Maria, Mary
Maritje	Mary
Mariken	Mary
Marregante	Magdalena
Marritius	Morice

Dutch/Frisian	English
Martijn	Martin
Martijntje	Martina
Mattheus	Matthew
Matthys	Matthew
Maybe	Maria, Mary
Mayken	Maria, Mary
Mayacca	Mary
Meewes	Bartholomew
Menassus	Myndert
Metje	Matilda
Metjen	Martha
Michiel	Michael
Micheltjen	Michael
Mie	Mary
Mietje	Mary
Mijntje	Wilhelmina, Mimmi
Morice	Maurice (but in at least one instance, Maria)
Na	Nanncy
Naatje	Anne
Neeltje	Cornelia
Niesje	Dionyse
Nol	Arnold
Obadja	Obadiah
Olivier	Oliver
Oeycke	Agnes
Oetje	Agnes
Orselina	Ursula
Outie	Agnes
Paultje	Paulina
Paylyntie	Pauline
Phlip	Philip
Piet	Peter
Pieter	Peter
Pietje	Petronella
Pouw	Paul
Powles	Paul
Randolph	Randal
Reimond	Raymond
Reindert	Reynold
Reinier	Reynold
Reinoud	Reynold
Resyntje	Rosina
Rijkaard	Richard
Rijkerd	Richard
Rip	Rupert
Ritsert	Richard
Robbert	Robert
Roedolf	Rudolphus
Roeland	Rowland
Roelof	Rolph, Ralph
Rogier	Roger
Rolfe	Ralph
Rombout	Rumbold
Roosje	Roseta
Rozemond	Rosamund
Ruben	Reuben
Rut	Roger
Rutgert	Roger
Rutsjert	Richard
Rykaard	Richard
Saal	Solomon
Saam	Samuel
Saar	Sarah
Saartje	Sally
Sander	Alexander
Sanna	Susannah
Sanneke	Susanna
Santje	Susanna
Sannertje	Susanna
Sasze	Sara
Sefia	Sophia
Seletje	Cecilia
Selie	Cecilia
Servass	Gervas
Seytie	Cynthia
Shaan	Christian
Sierrity	Charity

Dutch/Frisian	English
Sijmen	Simeon
Simson	Samson
Sitske	Cynthia
Smiaa	Hezekiah
Staats	Eustace
Stans	Constance
Steven	Stephen
Stijntje	Christina
Stoffel	Christopher
Styntje	Christina
Taatje	Sara
Tanna	Anna
Tanneken	Anne
Teeuw	Matthew
Teeuwis	Matthew
Teunis	Anthony
Teuntje	Antonia
Thys	Matthias
Tiebout	Theobald
Tientje	Albertina
Tietje	Albertina
Tijmen	Timothy
Tijs	Matthias
Tiletje	Albertina
Tit, Tietje	Albertina
Tjaatje	Charity
Tjerck	Theodorick
Tobias	Toby
Toff	Christopher
Toffels	Christopher
Tomatius	Timothy
Tonjes	Anthony
Tonnes	Anthony

Dutch/Frisian	English
Tool	Anthony
Toon	Anthony
Toontje	Antoinette
Tressje	Theresa, Tracy
Trijn	Catherine
Trui	Gertrude
Truitje	Gertrude
Tryntje	Catharine
Tsassen	Christian
Tzisso	Christian
Tymen	Timothy
Urseltje	Ursula
Ury	George
Valentijn	Valentine
Veltje	Valentine
Willem	William
Willemintje	Wilhelmina
Willempje	Willy
Willemtje	Wilhelmina
Willemyn	Wilhelmina
Wim	William, Willy
Wimpje	Wilhelmina, Mimmi
Wout	Walter
Wouter	Walter
Wyntje	Wilhelmina, Mimmi
Ydtje	Ida
Yke	Agnes
Yzaak	Isaac
Zanneke	Susan
Zjarritjen	Charity

Appendix B

English names and their equivalents in Dutch and Frisian Baptismal Names

English	Dutch/Frisian
Abraham	Bram
Adam	Daam
Adelaide	Adelheyd; Alyd
Adeline	Letje
Adolphus	Dolf
Adrian	Adriaantje; Ariaan; Arie; Arriaantje
Adrienne	Adriance
Agatha	Aaghie; Aagje; Aagt; Agt
Agnes	Agnietje; Angeniete; Anghe; Eike; Ikee; Oetje; Oeycke; Outie; Yke
Alberic	Alberick
Albert	Aldert
Albertina	Tientje; Tietje; Tietje; Tiletje; Tit
Albertus	Bertus
Aletta	Els; Elsje
Alexander	Sander
Alice	Aaltje; Adda; Aeftje; Alerta; Daatje
Alida	Annatje
Alwin	Alewijn
Andrew	Andreas; Andries; Dries
Angelica	Engel; Engelina; Engeltje
Anna/Anne	Tanna; Annatje; Annechet; Anneken; Annetje; Antie; Antje; En; Naatje; Tanneken; Eyntje
Anthony	Teunis; Tonjes; Tonnes; Tool; Toon
Antoinette	Toontje
Antonia	Teuntje
Arabella	Beletje
Arnold	Arendt; Nol
Arthur	Aart; Aert

English	Dutch/Frisian
Austen	Augustijn
Awdry	Ethilrede
Baldwin/ Balldwin	Boldwijn; Boudewyn; Boudje
Balthazar	Balt; Baltje; Baltrus
Barbara	Barber; Bartje
Barent	Barent
Bartholomew	Bart; Bartel; Bartelmus; Maas; Meewes
Bathilde	Batje
Beatrice	Badeloch
Bernard	Barend; Bernd
Bernardina	Dientje; Dina
Blasius	Blaas
Boniface	Bonifaas
Bridget	Bregje
Catharine	Catrijn; Kaat; Katrijn; Tryntje; Trijn
Cecilia	Celia; Seletje; Selie
Charity	Sierrity; Tjaatje; Zjarritjen
Charles	Carel; Ceerles; Cheerelz; Karel; Kareltje
Charlotte	Lotje
Christian	Kersten; Korsten; Kris; Krischan; Kruschen; Shaan; Tsassen; Tzisso
Christina	Christyntje; Krisje; Kristel; Kristijntje; Stijntje; Styntje
Christopher	Christoffel; Stoffel; Toff; Toffels
Clare	Klaar; Klaartje
Clasine	Classje
Conrad	Coenraad; Coenraadt; Coen
Constance	Stans
Cornelia	Cheiltje; Kee; Keetje; Neeltje
Cornelius	Case; Cornellis; Kees; Keesje; Koris
Cornelius	Krelis; Krelius
Crispin	Crispijn
Cynthia	Seytie; Sitske
David	Daaf
Debora	Diewertje
Dionyse	Niesje
Dionysius	Denys
Dora	Dortchen
Dorothy	Door; Doortje; Dort

English	Dutch/Frisian
Egbert	Epje
Eleanoor	Lenoor
Elise	Lezart
Elizabeth	Beth; Betje
Emily	Emmetje
Ephraim	Frem
Eustace	Staats
Eva/Efe	Aetje; Eefje; Ifje
Everard	Evert
Fanny	Francina
Florentina	Floortje; Florentijntje
Florian	Floris
Frances/Fanny	Femmetje; Francitjntje; Fransje
Francis	Frans
Frederic/ Frederick	Frits; Freek; Frerk; Friko
George	Goris; Joris; Jurgen; Jurian; Jurn; Jurrian; Jury; Ury
Geraldina	Gerritje
Gerarda	Geesje
Gerard	Garret; Geert; Gerrit
Gerardina	Desin
Gertrude	Geertie; Geertje; Geertrui
Gertrude	Geertruida; Geertruyd; Trui; Truitje
Gervas	Servass
Gilbert	Bert; Gijs; Gijsbertus; Gysbert; Gyslbert
Giles	Geleyn; Gellis
Godfrey	Godfried
Guy	Guido
Helena	Eelet; Heyltje
Henriette	Hendrica; Hendrikje; Hentje; Jetje
Henry	Enrik; Hein; Heintje
Hercules	Harck
Herman	Harmen; Manus
Hezekiah	Hiskia; Smiaa
Hilda	Hilletje; Hilligond
Hubert	Huybert
Hugo	Huigen
Ida	Eytic; Ydtje
Isaac	Yzaak

ENGLISH	DUTCH/FRISIAN
Isabella	Bell; Bella
Jack	Hans
Jackie	Hannes
Jacobina	Jacoba; Koosje
Jacob	Jaap; Jaapie; Jacobje; Jaepje; Japic; Joaptie; Jobje
Jacobus	Koba
James \ Jemmy \ Jem	Ko
James	Chime; Jacob; Jacobus
Jane	Jaantje; Janneken; Jannetje; Janotje; Jansje; Jantina
Jasper	Casper
Jemima	Jacomyntje
Jem/Jemmy	Ko
Jenny	Justje
Jeremiah	Jeremias
Jerome	Hieronimus; Jeronimus
Joachim	Jochem
Joan \ Johanna	Hansje
Johanna	Hansje
John/Jack/ Jackie	Hans; Hannes
John	Jan; Joannes; Johannes
Johnny	Jantje
Josine	Josyntje
Juliana	Juliaantje
Justin \ Joseph	Joost
Justin	Justin
Kate \ Kathleen	Katryntje
Kate \ Kitty	Kaatje
Kathleen	Katryntje; Kesia
Lambert	Lambrecht
Lawrence	Laurens; Louw
Leo	Lieve
Leonard	Leen; Leendert
Lewis	Lodewijk; Loures
Lisbet	Lijsbert; Lys; Lysbet
Lise	Lijsje; Lysje
Louis	Ludovicus
Lucy	Lucia

ENGLISH	DUTCH/FRISIAN
Luke	Lukas; Luytje
Madge	Griet
Magdalena/ Magdalen	Leentje; Lena; Marregante; Magdaleentje
Margaret	Griet; Margit; Margriet; Margrietje
Maria \ Mary	Mayken; Marij; Maybe
Martha	Metjen
Martina	Maartje; Martijntje
Martin	Maarten; Martijn
Mary	Maaicke; Marij; Mariken; Maritje; Mayacca; Maybe; Mayken; Mie; Mietje
Mathilda/ Matilda	Machteld; Magtelt; Metje
Matthew	Mattheus; Matthys; Teeuw; Teeuwis
Matthias	Thys; Tijs
Maurice	Morice
Meg	Grietje
Michael	Giel; Machiel; Micheltjen; Michiel
Mimmi	Mijntje; Wimpje; Wyntje
Morice	Marritius
Myndert	Menassus
Nancy	Na
Neeltje \ Cornelia	Beeltje
Nicholas \ Nick	Klaasje; Claes; Klaas
Obadiah	Obadja
Oliver	Olivier
Paulina/ Pauline	Paultje; Paylyntie
Paul	Pouw; Powles
Peg/Peggy	Griet; Grietje
Peter	Piet; Pieter
Petronella	Pietje
Philip	Phlip
Quirine	Kyrn
Rachel	Gepje
Ralph	Roelof; Rolfe
Randal	Randolph
Raymond	Reimond
Reuben	Ruben

English	Dutch/Frisian
Reynold	Reindert; Reinier; Reinoud
Richard	Rijkaard; Rijkerd; Ritsert; Rutsjert; Rykaard
Robert	Robbert
Roger	Rogier; Rut; Rutgert
Rolph \ Ralph	Roelof
Rosamund	Rozemond
Roseta	Roosje
Rosina	Resyntje
Rowland	Roeland
Rudolphus	Roedolf
Rumbold	Rombout
Rupert	Rip
Sally	Saartje
Samson	Simson
Samuel	Saam
Sarah/Sara	Saar; Sasze; Taatje
Sebastian	Bastian
Simeon	Sijmen
Solomon	Saal
Sophia	Fick; Fletje; Fytje; Sefia
Stephen	Steven
Susannah/ Susanna	Sann; Sanneke; Sannertje; Santje
Susan	Zanneke
Theobald	Tiebout
Theodore	Dorus
Theodoric	Deerick; Dierderick; Dirk; Dirkje; Tjerck
Theodosia	Doostie
Theresa	Tressje
Timothy	Goverd; Tijmen; Tomatius; Tymen
Toby	Tobias
Tracy	Tressje
Ursula	Orselina; Urseltje
Valentine	Valentijn; Veltje
Walter	Wout
Walter	Wouter
Wilhelmina	Mimmi; Mijntje; Wyntje; Wimpje; Willemintje; Willemtje; Willemyn
William	Wim; Willem
Willy	Willempje; Wim

Appendix C

Truncated and Superscripted Names

Names that have been superscripted can be a puzzle. There may be several variations used for the same name. Some of the more commonly used versions follow.

Superscript	Name
$Abig^{l}$	Abigail
Ab^{n}; A^{ner}	Abner
Ab^{r}; Abr^{m}	Abraham
Ag^{n}	Agnes
$Alex^{r}$	Alexander
And^{r}	Andrew
$Anth^{n}$	Anthony
$Arch^{d}$	Archibald
$Barn^{s}$	Barnabus
$Barth^{w}$	Bartholomew
Ben^{j} or $Benj^{m}$	Benjamin
Ber^{d}	Bernard
$Cath^{ne}$	Catherine
Chas or Chas	Charles
$Cath^{ne}$; $Cath^{n}$	Catherine
$Corn^{l}$	Cornelius
Cyr^{n}	Cyrenus
Danl	Daniel
Dav^{d}	David
Deb^{r}	Deborah
Der^{k}	Derrick
Dom^{k}	Dominick
$Doro^{y;}$ Dor^{o}	Dorothy
$Eben^{r}$	Ebenezer
Edm^{d}	Edmund
Edwd	Edward
$Eliph^{t}$	Eliphalet

Eliz^{a}; Elizth	Elizabeth (note that Eliza, not superscripted, can be the given name and not shortened for Elizabeth)
Em^{l}	Emanuel
Em^{l}	Emily
Esth^{r}	Esther
Eug^{ne}	Eugene
Ez^{r}	Ezra
Fra^{s}; Fran^{s}	Francis
Fred^{k}	Frederick
Gwen^{d}	Gwendolyn
H^{y}; Hen^{y}	Henry
Ja^{s}	James
Jno	John
Jo^{s}	UsuallyJoseph/Josephus; watch for possibility of Josiah or Joshua
J^{er}	Jeremiah
Jr^{o}	Jerome
Law^{r}	Lawrence
Lem^{l}	Lemuel
Leon^{d}	Leonard
Matt^{h}	Matthew
Mt^{g}	Montgomery
Nathl	Nathaniel
Nich^{s}	Nicholas
Reb^{a}	Rebecca
Saml	Samuel
Theo^{s}	Theophilus
Thos	Thomas
Tim^{o}	Timothy
Trist^{m}	Tristram
Wash^{n}	Washington
W^{m}	William
X^{er}, Xs^{ter}	Christopher
Zach^{r}	Zachariah
Zach^{y}	Zachary
Zep^{h}	Zephaniah

APPENDIX D

Male/Female Names

The following given names were used for both males and females. Some are still so used, though less frequently. The following list does not include the numerous *nicknames* that can appear for both male and female, such as Franky for Francis or Frances. Those nicknames can be found in the nicknames listings earlier in Sections A and B in this book.

Note also that many nicknames can be either for a female name, or for a male name, though the *full* names can differ. For example, Bobbie can be a female named Barbara or Roberta, or a male named Robert. Frankie can be for a female named Frances, or a male named Francis or Franklin; Chris for a female named Christine or a male named Christopher, etc. If the name on the record is a shortened name or nickname, study it and associated records carefully to determine whether it is a male or female. (See Sections 1 and 2.)

SAME SOUNDING (OR SPELLED) NAMES FOR MALE AND FEMALE

Alma
Beverl(e)y
Berneice/Bernice
Carol/Carroll
Comfort
Connie
Deliverance
Doris/Dorris
Earle (males can use this spelling too)
Eleanor, Ellener/Elender
Estelle
Ethel
Evelyn
Experience
Fay, Faye
Frances/Francis

Gail/Gale
Gene/Jean
Hillery
Jesse, Jessie
Jody
Joyce
June
Kay
Kelly
Laverne
Leslie/Lesley
Marian/Marion
Michael/Michal
Mildred
Pearl
Shirley
Sydney/Sidney
Valentine

Appendix E

Nicknames in New England

by Donald Lines Jacobus, M.A., F.A.S.G.

The following writing of Mr. Jacobus is reprinted from "Nicknames in New England," *The American Genealogist,* 45 (April 1969): 78-81 with comments appended at the end of the article by the then editor, George E. McCracken, Ph.D., F.A.S.G.

The changes undergone by given names are almost incredible and some seem utterly unreasonable. There is plenty of evidence that nick-names and pet names were used in England from an early period, and in New England as well, though here they appear only occasionally in official records and church registers in Puritan communities until we get well into the 18th Century. They have blossomed out, however, from then until the present day, and the more popular nicknames have often been bestowed on children as their proper names.

Many of these nicknames involve nothing more than abbreviating the full name, using only the first syllable, such as Tom or Thomas and Dave for David, and we shall pass these over as self-explanatory. Possibly the oddest nicknames were those which altered the initial letter of the name or placed a letter in front of a shortened form of the name. There was, for example, a notable tendency to place the letter 'n' in front of names beginning with a vowel. Thus, we have Ned (also Ted) for Edward, Nabby (as well as Abby) for Abigail, Nan and Nancy for Ann or Anna, and Nell and Nellie for Ellen, Eleanor and Helen. I do not recall seeing Noll used for Oliver in New England, though it may have been, for Garrick, in his poetic description of the dramatist Oliver Goldsmith, wrote:

. . . . . for shortness call'd Noll

Who wrote like an angel and talk'd like poor Poll.

At least three nicknames substituted a 'p' for the initial letter 'm', namely, Patty (as well as Matty) for Martha, Peggy (as well as Meg) for Margaret and Polly (as well as Molly) for Mary. Today, Patty is mostly used as a shortened form for Patricia. Among masculine nicknames, it is hard to explain why Dick was used for Richard, Bob (as well as Rob) for Robert, and Bill or Billy for William. All three of these names start with a weak consonant, and substituting a harder, more explosive consonant may be due to the fact that very young brothers or sisters found it easier to use these consonants when trying to address an older brother, and that such "baby talk" was picked up and used by the older members of the family.

Curiously enough, I have seen two names beginning with 'l' changed and lengthened by the insertion of an initial 'e', namely, Elidia for Lydia and Elemuel for Lemuel. This was certainly not a common mutilation, and I am unable to explain it.

The use of Harry for Henry originated no doubt in anglicizing the French *Henri.* Hal has been used for both Henry and Harold. Relatives of my maternal grandparents called them "Uncle Hank" and "Aunt Mate." Their actual names were Henry and Mary Ann and they grew up in central New York State, where I understand Hank and Mate were common nicknames for Henry and Mary over a century ago.

Elizabeth produced a spate of nicknames for, in addition to Eliza and Beth, we find Betty, Betsey and Bessie. Hester was used for Esther, Becky for Rebecca, Sukey for Susan, Ike for Isaac, both Frank and Fanny for the feminine Frances, Sene (two syllables) for Asenath, Zeke for Ezekiel, Hattie for Harriet, Viny for Lavinia, and Lotta or Lottie for Charlotte. Louise or Louisa seems to have been considered sometimes as a long form of Lois, and Lovisa also occurs. There are indications that in Louisa and Lovisa the 'i' was long as in "ice." Hitty and Hetty are both found for Mehetabel (also spelled Mehitable and other ways); Mitty was also used for this name as well as for Submit. In olden times Dolly was the usual pet name for Dorothy, but probably Dotty or Dot are in more common use today. Kate, Kitty and Kathy were used for Katherine (Catherine), though Kathy now usually signifies Kathleen which was a most unusual named [*sic*] in colonial New England.

One curious feature of early nomenclature deserves special mention. It was common in England, and not unknown here, to end some feminine names with 'an.' Thus we find Lucian (Luciuana) for Lucy Ann,

Julian (Juliana) for Julia Ann, Adrian or Adrienne for Audrey or Adrea Ann, and most commonly Marian for Mary Ann. Only the last, spelled both Marian and Marion, is still in common use, as is also the French form, Marianne. Novices are often puzzled when they find that the grandmother of William Edwards, founder of the illustrious Edwards family, was named Julian, and that the wife of the Rev. Edward[2] Bulkeley was named Lucian, since today these would be taken for masculine names.

The suffix "ette" and "etta" by the late 18th century came to be added to some feminine names, as Juliet (Juliette), used by Shakespeare, from Julia, and Margaretta from Margaret. It was also used to convert some masculine names, as Henrietta from Henry and Georgette from George. The diminutive, used as a nickname, came into such common use as to be considered a given name in its own right–Etta. Although this may possibly have been an actual name earlier in use in England (a subject I have not investigated), it seems to have been unknown in New England until it began to appear as a diminutive. Annette was another name formed with this diminutive, and this produced the nickname Nettie, which I think was also used at times as a nickname for Etta. If so, it follows the tendency already described to place the letter 'n' in front of names beginning with a vowel.

Although the foregoing is admittedly a superficial introduction to the study of given names and nicknames in New England, it is felt nevertheless that it will be found helpful and suggestive to those who are puzzled by the name changes they encounter in their research.

Editor George E. McCracken's Notes added to the above article: The foregoing article is, indeed, suggestive and stimulates me to the following comments. The name Mehetabel often was contracted to Mabel. This is a school which would maintain that Harry is not always derived from Henry but has a right to its own existence. There is also the nickname Humie, born by a young woman in an English family on Long Island in the 17th century, derived, it is supposed, from Posthuma, a name indicating the youngest daughter or a daughter born posthumously. The 'h' in this name intruded in late Latin on the mistaken notion of a connection with humare, to bury, or humus, earth, but that remarkable lady, the first wife of William Penn, was Gullena Maria Postuma Springett, the correct Latin form of the word for 'last' being regularly found. Her name was also remarkable for being made of more than one word, in this case commemorating the deceased father, Sir William Springett, who never knew his daughter, and the mother Mary Proude. I can think of only one example as early as this and it is even earlier, namely, Martha Johannah Winthrop, only child of Henry Winthrop by his wife Elizabeth Fones, later wife of Robert Feake and, perhaps, of William Hallett. Documents in the Winthrop papers prove this name, though the double name was rare even in the 18th century, e.g. Charles Brockden Brown, the novelist. As for Julian, we can cite a still earlier example, namely Julian of Norwich, the Benedictine nun who is famous as a mystic, but *The Dictionary of National Biography* insists on calling her Juliana. Juliana is alleged to have been born in 1343 and died in 1443.

Appendix F

English equivalents of Italian names, Nicknames, and Diminutives

The core list is used with permission of Ken Johnston, who tells us that he compiled it with the assistance of a number of others, including some members of PIE (POINTers in EMail). Some additions and regrouping was made. Some that were the same or so similar that only one letter differed were omitted, and some where the equivalent was not English were omitted. Some that are listed are nicknames (such as Gina for Regina), and some are diminutives (such as Ciccio for Francisco or Marietta for Maria).

Italian	English equivalent, nickname, or diminutive
Abramo	Abraham
Achille	Achilles
Adamo	Adam
Addolorata\ Dolorada	Dolores (derived from Our Lady of Sorrow)
Adelina	Adeline
Adriano	Adrian
Agata	Agatha
Agnese	Agnes
Agnesina	Aggie
Agostino	Austin, Augustin, Augustus
Alba, Albina	Dawn
Alberto	Albert
Aldo	Donald
Alesio	Alesis
Alessandrino	Alex, Alec
Alessandro	Alexander
Alfonso	Alphonse
Alfredo	Alfred
Alicia	Alice
Aloisio	Aloysius [sometimes Louis]
Ambrogio	Ambrose
Anatina	Anna, Antonia
Andrea	Andrew

Andreuccio	Andy
Angelina	Angeline
Aniello	Neil
Anna	Ann, Anne
Annetta	Annette, Annie, Nancy
Annina	Annie, Nancy
Anselmo	Anselm
Antonio	Anthony, Antoine, Anton
Araldo	Harold
Arnaldo	Arnold
Aronne	Aaron
Arrigo	Henry
Artur	Arthur
Augusto	August
Baldasarre	Balthazar
Baldovino	Baldwin
Cecilia	Cicily
Cecilio	Cecil
Celestina	Celeste
Celestino	Celestin
Cesare	Caesar
Chiara	Clair, Claire, Clare, Clara
Chirro	Cyril, Cyrus
Ciccio	diminutive of Francisco
Cipriano	Cyprian
Clairice	Clarissa
Claudiano	Claudian
Claudio	Claud, Claude
Clemente	Clement
Clemenza	Clemenze, Clementine
Cloe	Chloe
Coccino	diminutive of Francisco
Concella	Constance, Connie
Corinna	Corinne
Cornelio	Cornelius, Neil
Corradino\ Corrado	Conrad
Cosimo	Cosmo, Cosmos
Costanza	Constance
Costanzo	Constantine
Crescenza	Grace

Cristiano	Christian
Cristina	Christine
Cristoforo	Christopher
Dafne	Daphne
Damiano	Damian
Damone	Damon
Daniele	Daniel
Dario	Darien, Darius
Davide	David
Davidino	Davy
Demetrio	Demetrius
Desiderio	Desi, literally "desired"
Diana	Diane
Dionigi	Dennis
Dolorada	see Addolorata
Domenica	Dominique, Mae
Domenico	Dominic
Donato	Dan, Don, Donatus
Doride	Doris
Dootea	Dorothy
Durante	Durand
Edgardo	Edgar
Editta	Edith
Edmondo	Edmund
Edoardo	Edward
Egidio	Giles
Elena	Ellen, Helen, Helena
Elenora	Eleanor, Elinor
Elia	Eli, Elias
Elisa	Elise, Eliza
Elisabetta	Elisabeth, Elizabeth
Eloisa	Eloise, Elvira, Vera
Emilio	Amelia, Emilia, Emily
Emilio	Emile
Enrichetta	Harriet, Hatty, Henny, Henrietta, Hetty, Rita
Enrico	Henry
Erberto	Herbert
Erico	Eric
Erminia	Hermina
Erminio	Herman
Ermione	Hermione

Ernestina	Ernestine
Ernesto	Ernest
Esmondo	Esmond
Ester	Esther
Ettore	Hector
Eugenia	Eugenie, Jennifer
Eugenio	Eugene, Gene
Eva	Eva, Eve
Evelina	Evelyn
Ezechiele	Ezekiel
Fabiano	Favian
Fabrizio	Fabricius
Fausto	Faust
Federica	Frederica
Federico	Fred, Frederick
Felice	Felix
Felicia	Felice, Phyllis
Feliciano	Felicius
Felicita	Felicity
Feo	(might be from Federico)
Ferdinando/ Fernando	Ferdinand
Fifo	Raffaele
Filemone	Philemon
Filippa	Fannie
Filippo	Philip
Filomena	Philomena
Fiora	Flora
Fioralba	Dawn
Fiorenza	Florence
Flaviano	Flavian, Flavius
Fortunata	Fortune
Franca	Francie
Francesca	Frances
Francesco	Francis, Frank
Franco	Frank
Fulvio	Fulvius
Gabriele	Gabriel
Gaetana	Ida
Gaetano	Guy, Thomas
Geltrude	Gertrude

Gennaro	Gerald
Genoveffa	Geneva, Genevieve (often Jennie)
Geraldina	Geraldine
Geraldo	Gerald
Gerardo	Gerard
Geronimo	Jerome (In Latin records, Hieronimus)
Gervasio	Gervase
Giacinta/ Giacinto	Hyacinth
Giacoma	Jenny
Giacobbe	Jacob
Giacomina	Jackie, Jaclyn, Jenny
Giacomo	Jacques, James
Giampietro	John Peter
Gian-Andrea	John Andrew
Gian-Carlo	John Charles
Gian-Lorenzo	John Lawrence
Gianetta	Jeanette, Jenny
Gianetto	Jack
Gianmaria	John Marion
Gianni	Johnny
Giano	Ian
Giasone	Jason
Gilberto	Gilbert
Gina	Regina
Gino	Gene
Gioacchino	Joachim
Gioconda	Jocunda
Gionata	Jonathan
Giordana	Jordan
Giorgetto	Georgie
Giorgiana	Giorgiana, Giorgiane, Giorgianne
Giorgio	George
Giosi	Giuseppa
Giovanna	Jane, Joan, Joannna, Johanna
Giovanni	John
Giovannina	Jean
Girolama	Gerry, Mamie
Giuditta	Judith
Giulia	Julia, Julie
Giuliana	Juliana

Giulioano	Julian
Giulietta	Juliet
Giulio	Jules, Julius
Giuseppe	Joseph
Giuseppa \ Giussepina	Josepha, Josephine
Giustina	Justina
Giustiniano	Justinian
Giustino	Justin
Goffredo	Godfrey
Grazia	Grace
Gregorio	Gregory
Gualtiero	Walter
Guglielmino	Bill
Guglielmo	William
Guido	Guy
Guntero	Gunther
Gustavo	Gustav, Gustave
Ignasco	Ignace
Ilbario	Hilary
Iolanda	Yolanda
Isabella	Isabella, Isabel
Isacco	Isaac
Ivone	Yves
Lamberto	Lambert
Lea	Leah
Leandro	Leander
Lele	Gabriele
Lena	Magdalena, Maddalena, Pasqualena
Leonara	Lenore, Leonore
Leonardo	Leonard
Leone	Leo
Leopoldo	Leopold
Letizia	Leticia
Lia	Rosalia
Libera, Libero	Free, but often translated as Lee
Lidano	Leo
Lidia	Lydia
Lionello	Lionel
Lisa	Betty
Lisetta	Betsy

Lodovico	Lewis, Ludwig
Lorena	Lorraine
Lorenzo	Lawrence
Luca	Lucas, Luke
Lucano	Lucan
Lucia	Lucy, Lucia
Luciano	Lucian, Lucas
Lucrezio	Lucretius
Luigi	Louis
Luigia/Luisa	Louisa, Louise
Maddalena	Madeleine, Madeline, Magdalena
Magda	Maud
Manfredo	Manfred
Manlio	Manlius
Manuele	Emanuel, Manuel
Marcantonio	Mark Anthony
Marcellina	Marcelline, Marcy
Marcellino	Marcellinus
Marcello	Marcel, Marcellus
Marco	Mark
Margherita	Margaret, Margery, Madge, Margot, Marguerite
Maria	Maria, Marie, Mary
Marianna	Marianna, Marianne
Marietta	Marion, May, Peggy (and diminutive of Maria)
Mario	Marius
Marta	Martha
Martino	Martin
Massimiliano	Maximilian
Massimo	Max
Matilde	Mathilda
Matteo	Matthew
Mattia	Matthew, Matthias
Maurizio	Maurice
Mercede	Mercedes
Michele	Michael
Michelino	Mike
Mena, Mimma, Mina	Domenica
Meno, Mimmo, Mino	Domenico

Modesto	Modestus
Monica	Monique (or Monica)
Nannetta	Nancy, Nannette
Nardo	Bernardo, Leonardo
Natale	Noel
Natalia	Natalie
Nataniele	Nathan, Nathaniel
Nicoletta	Nicoletta, Nicole
Nicolo	Nicholas
Nicoluccio	Nick
Nina	Nan
Nina\ Ninuccia	"Baby," diminutive of many names
Nino	"Baby" could be applied to a number of names
Nunzia\ Nunzio	see Annunciata
Ofelia	Ophelia
Olivia	Olive, sometimes Lee
Oliviero	Oliver
Omero	Homer
Onofredo	Humphrey
Onofrio	perhaps Humphrey
Onorato	Honore
Orazio	Horace, Horatio
Orsola	Ursula
Ortensia	Hortense, Hortensia
Osvaldo	Oswald
Ovidio	Ovid
Paola	Paula
Paolina	Paulina
Paolino	Paulinus (possibly also Linus)
Paolo	Paul
Pasquale	Pascal, Patrick, Patsy
Patrizia	Patricia
Patrizio	Patrick
Perrino	Perry
Pietro, Piero	Peter
Pietruccio	Pete
Pindaro	Pindar
Pippo	Filippo, sometimes Giuseppe
Placidia	Pleasantine

Platone	Plato
Plinio	Pliny
Pompeo	Pompey
Porzia	Portia
Prospero	Prosper
Proteo	Proteus
Prudenza	Prudence
Quintino	Quintin
Rachele	Rachel
Raffaele	Ralph, Raphael
Raimondo	Raymond
Rainero	Rainerd, Reiner
Randolfo	Randolph
Raulo	Ralph
Rea	Rhea
Regina	Gina, Jean, Jenny
Reginaldo	Reginald
Reinardo	Reinhard
Renato	Renatus
Renzo	Lorenzo
Riccardo	Richard
Rina	Caterina
Rinaldo	Reggie, Reginald, Reynold, Ronald
Rita	Margherita
Roberto	Robert
Rodolfo	Ralph, Rudolph
Rodrigo	Roderic, Roderick
Rolando	Roland
Romolo	Romulus
Rosa	Rosa, Rose
Rosalinda	Rosalind
Rosamonda	Rosamund
Rosaria	Rose, Sadie, Sara
Rosario	Ross, Roy, Sal, Russ
Rosina	Rosalie, Rosie
Rossanna	Roxanne
Rufo	Rufus
Ruggero	Roger
Salamone	Solomon
Salvatore	Sal, often Sam
Samuele	Samuel

Sandra	Alessandra
Sandro	Alessandro, Andrew
Sansone	Samson
Santa, Santo, Santina	all derived from "saint"
Sara	Sarah, Sally
Saverio	Sam, Xavier
Savino	Sam
Santa, Santo, Santina	Rosaria
Saverio	Sam, Xavier
Savino	Sam
Sebastiano	Sebastian
Sibilla	Sibyl
Sigfrido	Siefried
Sigismondo	Sigmund
Silvestro	Silverter
Silvia	Sylvia
Simeone	Simeon
Simone	Simon
Siro	Cyril, Cyrus
Sofia	Sophie
Steefania	Stephanie
Stefano	Stephen, Steven
Stella	Estelle
Susetta	Susie
Taddeo	Thaddeus
Teo	perhaps Matteo
Teobaldo	Theobald
Teodato	Theodatus
Teodora	Theodora
Teodoro	Theodore
Terenzio	Terence
Teresa	Teresa, Theresa, Therese
Tibaldo	Tybald
Timoteo	Timothy
Tirone	Tyrone
Tito	Titus
Tommasino	Tom
Tommaso	Thomas
Toni	Antonio

Tonio	Antonio
Toto	Antonio, Salvatore
Turridu	Salvatore
Ubaldo	Hubaldus
Umberto	Hubert
Ugo	Hugo
Ulisse	Ulysses
Umberto	Humberto
Urania	Ron
Urbano	Urban
Valentino	Valentine
Valeria	Valerie
Valerieano	Valerian
Venere	Venus
Vilfrido	Wilfred
Vincenza	Vincentia
Vincenzius	Vinny
Vincenzo	Vincent
Vinfrido	Winfred
Viola	Violet
Virgilio	Virgil
Vittore	Vic, Victor
Vittoria	Victoria
Vittoriano	Victorian
Vittorio	Victor
Viviana	Vivian
Zaccaria	Zachary
Zenone	Zeno